When Dad Comes H[...]

MW00445329

written by Bryce and Noah with Taneshia Knight Shelton

When Dad Comes Home

Copyright ©2017 by Taneshia Knight Shelton

Illustrations ©2017 by Amariah Rauscher

All rights reserved. This book or any portion thereof may not be reproduced or used in any manner whatsoever without the express written permission of the author except for the use of brief quotations in a book review.

ISBN-10: 0996850325

ISBN-13: 978-0996850322

Library of Congress Control Number: 2017909531

The text of this book is set in Designer Notes font.

The illustrations in this book were created using watercolor and charcoal.

For all of the families waiting for mom or dad to come home.

Hello! I am Bryce and this is my little brother Noah! We have a Dad that is totally rad. He takes care of us and mom, too. He has a job that is really cool.

He is a Sailor in The Unites States Navy!
He wears blue uniforms and rides big ships.

He made a promise to serve, support, and defend this country we live in.
So, he has to leave us every now and then; sometimes, for months on end. Every
now and then, the ship will dock at a port. He helps those in need and provides
comfort to people just like you and me.

He works with gadgets, big and small, right there on the ship from dusk to dawn.

When he has to leave us, we get sad, but it's not too bad because when he returns we will have lots of fun! He will tell us all about the adventures he went on. We will tell him how well we took care of mom.

We will play with his ears and rub on his nose. We will hug our Dad and show him lots of love.

He will show us all the souvenirs he collected from shore to shore.

We will show him all the toys we talked mom into buying us while he was gone.

He will tell us about the new friends and memories he made.

We will tell him about the games we made up and played.

We will jump up and down like little clumsy clowns.

We will play in the dirt and mess up our shirts.

We will shoot lots of hoops and throw the football.

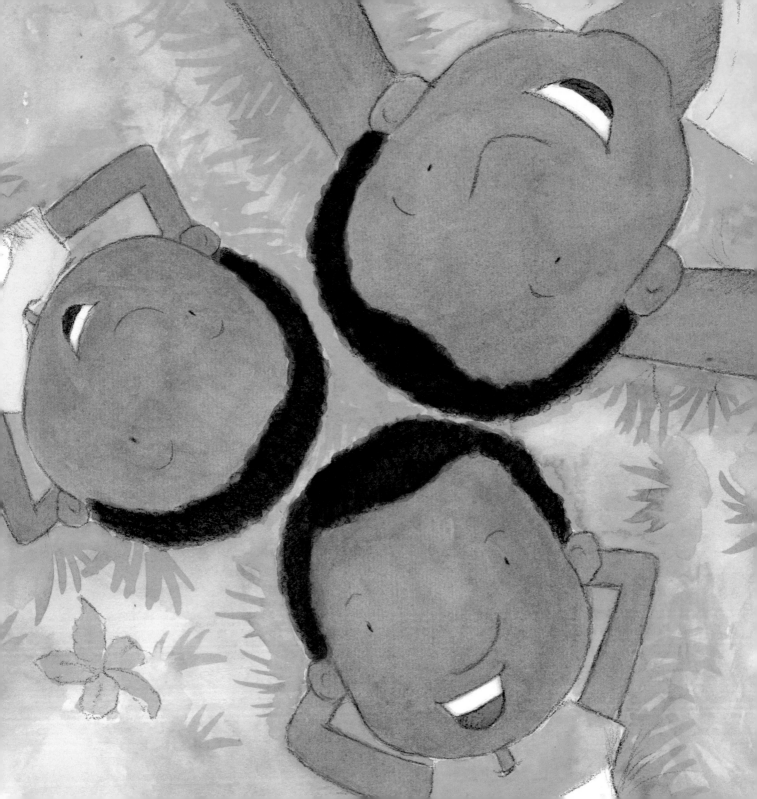

We will make up silly jokes and sing crazy songs.

We will have races and play hide and seek in our yard.

We will build a fort and camp out in our backyard. We will tell scary stories while eating s'mores around the camp fire.

We will wrestle and fight and do all of the things our mom doesn't like until we fall asleep under the stars.

All of these things we can't wait to do. But, until then, we will just play, pray, and wait for that very special day. The day our Dad returns and holds us in his arms!

Until they all come home.

Bryce and Noah resides in Maryland with their parents. When not in school, they enjoy reading, video games, and listening to music. They plan to keep their Dad busy now that he has made it back home.

46204683R00023

Made in the USA
Middletown, DE
25 July 2017